Learn **French** with

Max et Mathilde

En Vacances – On Holiday

A catalogue record for this book is available from the British Library

Published by Ladybird Books Ltd
80 Strand, London, WC2R 0RL
A Penguin Company

2 4 6 8 10 9 7 5 3 1

Image credits: page 13 Philip Gatward © Dorling Kindersley,
page 19: Paul Harris and Anne Heslope © Dorling Kindersley

ISBN: 978-140930-188-2

Printed in China

A few tips for grown-ups!

The most practical and enjoyable way to learn French with
Max et Mathilde is to listen to the CD and read along, listening
carefully to the pronunciation and then repeating the phrases.

Listen to the CD more than once. Repetition and singing along
will reinforce the vocabulary and phrases in the book.

Let the pictures guide your child. A translation appears at the back of the
book rather than on the page itself to avoid word-for-word translation.

On the right-hand page, the dialogue delivered by Max et Mathilde
is just as French children would speak to each other.

The most important thing is to maintain your child's enthusiasm, motivation
and interest in learning French. Above all, keep it simple and fun!

"Bonjour"

Viens en vacances avec nous! Nous allons au bord de la mer. Tu vas t'amuser!

"Je m'appelle Max."

"Je m'appelle Mathilde."

"Notre chien s'appelle Noisette!"

La valise

Max et Mathilde
partent en vacances.
Ils font leurs valises.

"Youpi!
C'est enfin
les vacances!"

Max

Noisette

"Maman, ma valise est trop petite.
Elle ne ferme pas!"

7

La voiture

Ils partent en voiture.
Tout le monde est prêt.

L'hôtel

Max et Mathilde arrivent à l'hôtel.
Ils ont chaud. Ils veulent
aller à la plage tout de suite.

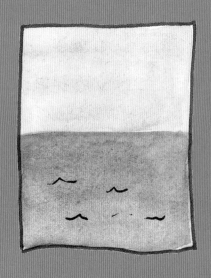

La mer

L'hôtel est à côté de la mer.
Les enfants font du kayak.

La plage

Les enfants adorent la plage.
Ils font des pâtés de sable.

Le restaurant

Chaque soir Max et Mathilde
dînent au restaurant
avec maman et papa.

La glace

C'est le dernier
jour des vacances.
Les enfants prennent
une glace avant de partir.

Translation

"Bonjour!" "Hello!"

Viens en vacances aves nous! Come on holiday with us!

Nous allons au bord de la mer. We're going to the seaside.

"Tu vas t'amuser!" "You'll have fun!"

"Je m'appelle Max." "I'm called Max."

"Je m'appelle Mathilde." "I'm called Mathilde."

"Notre chien s'appelle Noisette!" "Our dog's called Noisette!"

La valise The suitcase

Max et Mathilde partent en vacances. Max and Mathilde are going on holiday.

Ils font leurs valises. They're packing their suitcases.

"Youpi! C'est enfin les vacances!" "Hurrah! The holidays are here at last!"

"Maman, ma valise est trop petite." "Mum, my suitcase is too little."

"Elle ne ferme pas!" "It won't close!"

La voiture The car

Ils partent en voiture. They're going by car.

Tout le monde est prêt. Everyone's ready.

"Vite, Noisette! Tu pars aussi en vacances aves nous!"
"Quick, Noisette. You're coming on holiday with us, too!"

L'hôtel The hotel

Max et Mathilde arrivent à l'hôtel. Max and Mathilde arrive at the hotel.

Ils ont chaud. They're hot.

Ils veulent aller à la plage tout de suite. They want to go straight to the beach.

"Dépêche-toi, Max!" "Hurry up, Max!"

"Mais où est mon maillot de bain?" "But where are my swimming trunks?"

La mer The sea
L'hôtel est à côté de la mer. The hotel is by the sea.
Les enfants font du kayak. The children are kayaking.
"Je vais plus vite que toi, Max!" "I'm going faster than you, Max!"
"Mais je te rattrape." "But I'm catching up with you."

La plage The beach
Les enfants adorent la plage. The children love the beach.
Ils font des pâtés de sable. They are making sand-castles.
"Fais attention, Noisette!" "Be careful, Noisette!"

Le restaurant The restaurant
Chaque soir Max et Mathilde dînent au restaurant avec maman et papa.
Every evening Max and Mathilde eat supper in a restaurant with Mum and Dad.
"Que désirez-vous?" "What would you like?"
"Une pizza, s'il vous plaît, monsieur." "A pizza, please!"

La glace The ice cream
C'est le dernier jours des vacances. It's the last day of the holidays.
Les enfants prennent une glace avant de partir.
The children are having an ice cream before leaving.
"Au revoir! À l'année prochaine." "Bye-bye. See you next year."

Holiday Phrases

Bonjour! Hello!

Bonsoir! Good evening!

Au revoir! Goodbye!

À bientôt! See you soon!

Où est...? Where is...?

Où est la plage? Where is the beach?

Où est l'hôtel? Where is the hotel?

Où est le restaurant? Where is the restaurant?

Où est la piscine? Where is the swimming pool?

Allons à la plage. Let's go to the beach.

Allons au restaurant. Let's go to the restaurant.

J'ai faim. I'm hungry.

J'ai soif. I'm thirsty.

Je voudrais... I would like...

Je voudrais une glace à la vanille.
I'd like a vanilla ice cream.

Je voudrais une glace au chocolat.
I'd like a chocolate ice cream.

Je voudrais un coca. I'd like a cola.

Je voudrais une pizza. I'd like a pizza.

J'adore nager. I love swimming.

Moi aussi! Me too!

Rentrons... Let's go back...

Rentrons à l'hôtel. Let's go back to the hotel.

Now listen to us on the CD.
We'll say everything in French and English, and then
you can try repeating. Afterwards, we can sing
the holiday song together!

Max et Mathilde's Holiday Song

Nous partons pour les vacances!
Nous allons nous amuser.
Nous allons manger des glaces
Montons vite dans la voiture!

Les vacances en plein soleil,
Les vacances en plein soleil!

Nous n'allons plus à l'école,
Nous allons nous amuser.
Nous partons pour les vacances!
Montons vite dans la voiture!

Les vacances en plein soleil,
Les vacances en plein soleil!

We're going off on holiday!
We're going to have fun.
We're going to eat ice creams
Quick, get in the car!

Holidays in the sunshine,
Holidays in the sunshine!

We're not going to school any more,
We're going to have fun.
We're going off on holiday!
Quick, get in the car!

Holidays in the sunshine,
Holidays in the sunshine!